Inner Magic

Pearls of Wisdom

The Magic of Me Series - Book Two

Inner Magic

Pearls of Wisdom

Your unique magic
lies within . . . .

Janie Emerson

ISBN: 978-0-9716320-5-9
Book design by Janie Emerson
Printed in the United States of America.

JEM Enterprises
La Jolla, California

ShamrockWisdom.com

DEDICATED TO

Our own inner magic

May we each be who and
what we want to be now
and forever -

Know your power and
live your inner magic
everyday....

INTRODUCTION

Unlock your Inner Magic

Magic is what transforms the seemingly ordinary into the truly special. It is by looking within that we see the true magic of who we are. It gives us the power to become our best. We reflect that "inner magic" in all we do each day.

Make this book a special part of your daily ritual. It is most powerful when used from a quiet, peaceful, loving space. Select your passage. Let it guide you within. Reflect its power all day.

This special book is given with love as your window to you.

See your "Inner Magic."

Your
own unique
magic
lies within . . . .

Your
power
comes from
within —

Expect
miracles
every
day —

Trust
your
knowing —

The key
is
to focus
on
the result
you
want . . . .

Just
be still
&
all is
clear —

In
the silence
I
receive
my answers

I am

happy

&

content

to

be me —

life
takes courage —

The
quiet internal
courage
of
me —

Your
clarity brings
new
opportunities
to
you —

I am
powerful
&
follow
my guidance
quietly . . . .

You
are limitless —
Create
your miracles
now . . . .

Let
others be
on
their paths
&
me be
on mine —

Being
successful means
enjoying
all of
life . . . .

Love
and see
your
miracles
unfold . . . .

Release
worry —
Believe
&
it is so —

Freedom
is
something you
feel
within —

Growth
requires
quiet
to
become
strength —

Gentleness
has
a power
beyond
measure —

Be
patient
&
all will
be well . . . .

Touch
all with love
always —

Including
yourself . . . .

Dreams
are air
for
the soul —

Release the gunk
Cherish the wisdom
&
Enjoy the knowing —

I believe
&
trust in
me —

Our
path is to
capture
life's
joys . . . .

When
you love,
you
enjoy life
&
its great
results —

Do
things honoring
what
works for
you —

Believe

in

your vision

&

make it

your

reality —

It takes
quiet time
to
become
strong —

Time
to
be peaceful
&
centered —

With
clear intention
you
thrive . . . .

In
faith,
I
leave fear
behind . . . .

Truth
gives you
life's
road map —

Anything
can
be healed
with
love . . . .

Songs
are the
sunshine
in
my soul . . . .

I
love,
cherish,
&
nurture
me always —

The
understanding
soul
is
the key to
love —

We
see special
love,
clear thoughts
&
total health.

Rushing
is doing . . . .

To savor
is
to live
life —

Remember
all
the little things
that
give joy —

The
real key
is
to love
&
to enjoy life —

live
each day
with
joy, love
&
hope —

The
past gives
gifts
that pave
the
future —

Stay
within yourself —

You
are your
power!

Focus
on
your dreams.

They
protect you
always . . . .

Intend
miracles
&
manifest
dreams —

True
love is
within . . . .

It is
important to
believe
&
the gifts
will

come —

It is
all just
energy —
We create
what
we
truly want . . . .

Your
dreams live
forever . . . .

Be
You —
&
All
is
Well —

Believe it!!!

&

Own it!!!

ABOUT THE AUTHOR

JANIE EMERSON

Janie Emerson is the author of the successful *Appreciate Each Day, The Magic of Me, Guided By Animal Angels, Walking With Angels, My Special Girls. and My World.* Her writings appear in newspapers and magazines. She has won national awards for her poetry and is a respected consultant and acclaimed speaker.

The inspiration for her writings comes from life. Janie's work gives balance, insight and focus to life's events. Her intent is to empower and to enhance your life.

Janie lives in La Jolla, CA with her husband Bob and her beloved Westies. She has been an advocate for women owned businesses nationally and an active community leader.

Janie is currently working on two great new projects.

ShamrockWisdom.com

www.ingramcontent.com/pod-product-compliance
Lightning Source LLC
Chambersburg PA
CBHW040554010526
44110CB00054B/2676